HANDY HINTS
for the
HORSE PERSON

HANDY HINTS
for the
HORSE PERSON
Hundreds of Tips to Save Time and Money

Karen Bush

Skyhorse Publishing

Skyhorse Publishing books may be purchased in bulk at special discounts
for sales promotion, corporate gifts, fund-raising, or educational purposes.
Special editions can also be created to specifications. For details,
contact the Special Sales Department, Skyhorse Publishing, 307 West 36th
Street, 11th Floor, New York, NY 10018 or info@skyhorsepublishing.com.

www.skyhorsepublishing.com

10 9 8 7 6 5 4 3 2

Library of Congress Cataloging-in-Publication Data

Bush, Karen.
  Handy hints for the horse person : hundreds of tips to save time and
money / Karen Bush.
    p. cm.
  ISBN 978-1-61608-106-5
  1. Horses--Miscellanea. I. Title.
  SF285.B9768 2010
  636.1--dc22

                              2010022555

Printed in China

Introduction

More and more people are keeping horses and ponies of their own these days, and though you do not need to be tremendously wealthy in order to do so, it can still prove to be an expensive and time-consuming hobby. Obviously you should never consider attempting to economize on things that are essential to your horse's well-being, such as regular feeding, worming, shoeing, and veterinary attention, but there are a number of ways in which it is possible to save both time and money.

If you are new to horse or pony owning, you probably have not yet found out about many of these legitimate "shortcuts." Even if you are an experienced owner, it does not mean that you have stumbled across all of them. You will find that you keep discovering new ideas all the time—for as long as you continue to keep a horse, in fact. This book tries to give you at least a head start if you are a novice, or to nudge your memory if you are more knowledgeable, by setting down some practical hints and tips that will make life a little easier and your stable management more successful.

1   When trimming your horse's whiskers, save time and produce a neater result by using a plastic safety razor instead of scissors. It is also safer if he tends to fidget.

2   The seams of horse blankets and sheets often leak. Waterproof them effectively and cheaply by rubbing a piece of candlewax along the stitching.

3   Use a little aerosol furniture polish to produce a good shine on rubber boots.

4   To give a more professional touch to your blankets, add your initials to the nearside corner. Either buy the individual letters from a tack shop or from a needlework or craft shop, or make your own by drawing a paper template, pinning it on to a square of felt, and cutting around it. You can then stitch the letters into position.

5   If you keep losing your hoof pick in your horse's bedding, braid a piece of brightly colored baling string and tie it to the handle.

6   To make a white tail look really white again, wash it using a little laundry soap powder. Be careful not to get it on to the skin of the horse's tail dock, as it may irritate and cause rubbing.

7   When your velveteen-covered hunt cap becomes faded and scruffy, freshen it with an appropriately colored suede shoe spray.

8   Make an inexpensive feed scoop by cutting diagonally across an empty plastic quart or half-gallon bottle.

9   Use a piece of baling string to hang up a penknife or a pair of scissors near your supply of hay or straw, ready to cut open the bales.

10 Really hard blobs of grease on tack can be removed either with a fingernail or with a bunch of horsehair.

11   A plastic sink dish bowl makes a cheap and useful feed bowl that is also easy to clean.

12   Tie a knot in the end of your lead rope when leading your horse, so the rope does not slip through your hands. Wear gloves, too, so that if he tries to pull away you have a better grip. You'll also avoid burning the palms of your hands.

13   Remove bot fly eggs with a disposable plastic safety razor, far cheaper than buying a bot knife.

14   If your horse has a very greasy coat which spoils his appearance or makes him difficult to clip, tackle the worst areas by adding a little Dettol to a bucketful of warm water. Wring a sponge out in it, and then rub it vigorously against the direction the hair lies. Rinse frequently. You will see the grease beginning to form a scum on the top of the water as it comes out of the coat.

15   Use old saddle soap cans as bridle racks. Just nail them to the tack room wall. A rounded rack will help to keep bridles and halters in shape as well as keeping them neat.

16   If your horse paws the ground just inside his stall door, place a rubber mat there. It will prevent the toes of his shoes from being worn out quickly, and if he cannot hear the noise, he may stop. Turn him out as often as possible, too, in case the habit is caused by boredom.

17   Make your own hoof dressing by mixing a little pine tar into vegetable cooking oil.

18   Sell manure to mushroom farmers and nurseries, which will also keep your manure pile to a reasonable size. Negotiate the deal so the farmer or nursery-owner will haul the manure away.

19   Save old pieces of saddle soap that are too small to use. When you have enough, heat them gently in an old saucepan until they melt. Pour the liquid into an empty margarine container and leave it in the refridgerator until it hardens.

20   Putting worm powders into the refrigerator a day or two before you give them to your horse reduces the odor so the horse will not object.

21　It is cheaper to make your own hay nets out of baling string than to buy them. About twenty-four strings will make an average-sized net. Tie them all into a large knot, which can be hung from a nail. Then knot alternate pairs of strings together to complete one row. Knot pairs of strings together on the next row in a similar way, but using one each of the strings from the pairs knotted in the first row, so that large holes are formed. You can make these holes bigger or smaller, depending upon the distance apart that you make the knots. Continue in this way until the net is complete. When you have finished, braid some string together to make a drawstring.

22　Before going into the show arena, dab a little baby oil around your horse's eyes and muzzle to enhance his appearance. Leave this chore until the last moment, so that hair and dust do not stick to the oil.

23   If blanket and cooler leg straps tend to chafe, and if you have made sure they are kept clean and supple and are not too tight, try slipping a length of thin rubber tubing over them.

---

24   The cheapest antiseptic wash for cuts is salt water. Never use disinfectants for cleaning wounds as they will impede the healing process.

---

25   Vinegar makes a cheap fly repellent.

---

26   Never tie your horse directly to a stationary object. Always tie his lead rope to a break-able piece of string that will snap if he panics and pulls back, thus saving his halter—and his neck—from harm.

---

27 When washing girths in a washing machine, place them inside an old pillowcase to keep the buckles from doing any damage to the machine.

28 A large rubber ball in a paddock or pasture water trough will help prevent water from completely freezing over in winter, and will leave a drinking hole until you arrive to break the rest of the ice.

29 When your old lead rope wears out, make a new one by braiding some baling string and attaching it to the old clip.

30 A tail wrap or a length of pantyhose or a tights leg on your horse's tail while he is being clipped will keep the hairs safely out of the way of the clippers.

31   Put a few drops of baby oil on a soft brush and carefully brush through your horse's tail while it is clean. As well as helping to prevent tangles, the oil will also make the hairs less brittle and will help keep prevent white hairs from becoming discolored.

---

32   If scissors or a knife are not available, you can easily cut through the string on a bale of hay or straw by using another piece of string. Slip it beneath the strings and, holding an end in each hand, use a sawing motion to cut them through.

---

33   An old sleeping bag can easily be converted into a warm quilted stable blanket for the winter. Remove the zipper and cut out a semi-circular section at one end for the neck and shoulders. Stitch around the edges. Use strips of broad Velcro for breast straps.

34   Flies are attracted more to sweating and dirty horses than to clean ones, so bathe your horse regularly during the summer months. If the weather is warm, give him a quick sponge down after exercise. Shampoos with a mild antiseptic added also act as an additional protection against flies.

35   After an injury has healed up, the hair may not grow back in the affected area for some time. Stimulate growth by rubbing a little Vaseline into the skin.

36   A horse with a whispy forelock will benefit from a fly fringe to keep flies away from his eyes. Loop pieces of string around an old browband and attach it to the halter so it fits snugly. Check regularly under the browband for any signs of chafing.

37   Cribbing will be discouraged by smearing mustard on surfaces that your horse bites onto.

38   Use an old dish or hand towel as a stable rubber. This is less expensive than buying the real thing from a tack shop.

39   Cheaper than coat gloss for a gleaming finish on your horse's coat is a little aerosol furniture polish sprayed on a stable rubber and then wiped on. Warning: Try a small patch first just to check that there are no allergic reactions.

40   Remove the grease and dirt from your tack by using hot water with a little dish-washing liquid added to it. Saddle-soap afterwards, and oil the leather occasionally so that it remains supple.

41　To prevent a surcingle from rubbing or pressing on your horse's back, place a thick piece of sponge beneath it at the point where it crosses the spine.

42　When washing your horse, it is cheaper to use an economy-size brand of shampoo than a special equine preparation. However, try a small test area first to make sure that there is no allergic reaction.

43　If your horse keeps kicking over his water bucket in the stable, put it inside an old car tire.

44　Braided baling string hung across your tack room or feed shed makes a clothesline for wet blankets and coolers to dry.

45   If your horse is difficult to catch, try keeping a piece of crinkly paper in your pocket to arouse his interest and lure him close enough to be tempted by the carrot or sugar lump you also brought along.

46   Shampoo your horse's coat a day or so before a horse show or before he is to be looked at by a prospective buyer so that the coat has time to settle and regain its natural sheen for the big day. A mane that has been recently shampooed is also difficult to braid.

47   Brittle feet can be improved by adding a package of gelatin dissolved in a cupful of hot water to one feeding a day.

48 Disinfect secondhand saddlery or horse clothing thoroughly before use. If your tack should ever become moldy, disinfect it before using it again since fungal spores that are not killed by normal cleaning will cause a skin infection.

49 If your horse tends to finish his hay very quickly, buy or make him a hay net with smaller holes.

50 Provide some amusement for your horse when he is stabled by drilling a hole through a large turnip. Thread a piece of rope or braided baling string through the hole, then hang the turnip in his stall for him to nibble at.

51   Shoe whitener is effective on a horse's white socks for a halter, conformation, or showmanship class. Alternatively, use a block of white chalk or even talcum powder.

52   If you find that your crop, whip, or bat tends to slide through your hand because there is no knob on the handle, slip a rubber martingale stop over the top.

53   Sheepskin sadde pads can be kept reasonably clean if you sprinkle them with a little talcum powder after use and then gently brush it out. The power will absorb some of the sweat and dirt.

54 Linseed helps to promote a healthy bloom on the coat because it is rich in fats. It is easily digested and will help to put on weight. To feed, use twenty parts water to one part linseed. Soak for six hours, strain off the water, and replace with fresh water. Bring it to a boil in a heavy saucepan and simmer uncovered for four hours, stirring occasionally. This will form a thick jelly-like substance, a teacupful of which may be fed two or three times a week. Before feeding, check that the seeds have broken. Never feed uncooked linseed: the seeds are poisonous in their raw state.

55 Clean and keep old blankets and coolers instead of throwing them away. They can be cut up and used to repair tears in newer blankets and coolers.

56   How you braid a mane can do a lot to improve the appearance of your horse. Lots of small, dainty braids will make a short, thick neck look better proportioned, while fewer larger ones built up along the crest will make a long, thin neck appear to carry more muscle.

57   When turning a horse that you are holding, always turn him away from you so that he does not step on your toes. If you are showing him to a veterinarian or a prospective buyer or you are in a halter or showmanship class, you will not block the view of whoever is watching.

58   Trimming away a small section of mane just behind the ear makes the bridle headpiece sit better.

59 Codliver oil is cheaper to buy in a large gallon container than in a small bottle. If you want to use it as a feed additive to improve the quality of your horse's coat, split the cost and the oil with another horse-owning friend.

60 Leave long fetlock hairs untrimmed during wet winter months, as they will act as natural drainpipes, leading water away from the heel region and helping to prevent cracked heels. Heels can be further waterproofed by smearing a little Vaseline in them.

61 Billets are more easily undone by pushing the leather up into a loop so that it slides off the hook stud. That technique also prevents the leather in the area from becoming damaged and weakened—and it also reduces the likelihood of your breaking your fingernails.

62   Clean your grooming kit at the same time as you shampoo your horse so you don't brush dirt straight back into his coat.

63   Cobwebs will darken a stall and dusty ones can aggravate stable coughs. They should be cleared away regularly.

64   Overreach boots can sometimes cause chafing if the horse is unaccustomed to wearing them. Smear a little Vaseline around the tops so that they slide freely around the pastern.

65   Change the type of wormer you use once
     a year. Worms can build up a degree of
     immunity, and a wormer may become less
     effective after prolonged use. Do not simply
     change the brand, but check the ingredients
     on the label to make sure that the wormer
     contains a different anthelmintic.

66   Tying a hoof pick to an old bucket by a long
     piece of string will keep you from losing it,
     and will provide you with a container into
     which you can pick out your horse's feet
     so that you do not soil the stall, aisle, or
     ground.

67   When trimming the end of a tail, ask
     someone to place an arm underneath it so
     that it is in the position in which your horse
     carries it when moving. Otherwise, you may
     end up trimming it too short.

68   If you do not have a shovel or manure fork, scoop up piles of droppings between two pieces of board measuring about nine inches by twelve inches. Straw and hay can also be picked up in this way after they have been swept up into piles.

69   Oil the leather on blankets, coolers, and canvas girths before washing them, or apply a little Vaseline, so that water and detergent do not do any damage. Afterward, wash and saddle-soap the leather thoroughly.

70   If you mount from the ground, change your English saddle's stirrup leathers from one side of the saddle to the other frequently. This will prevent the one on the near (left) side from becoming stretched by being used for mounting all the time.

71   If your horse is a fussy feeder, oral medication can easily be given by placing it inside a hollowed-out apple or carrot. You can also mix powders and crushed tablets and pellets with molasses and smear it on the tongue with a wooden spoon so that your horse cannot spit it out.

---

72   Make a checklist of everything you will need to take with you to an event away from home and check off the items as they are loaded into your truck or trailer so that you do not forget anything.

---

73   Baling string can be used as an emergency sweat scraper by taking a doubled-up length and drawing it down across your horse's wet coat.

74   Water in buckets in a stall should be changed regularly. The ammonia that it absorbs from the stable atmosphere gives it an unpleasant taste that your horse might find objectionable. You also don't want to get algae buildup.

75   Check three or four times a year that your saddle fits correctly. Your horse's shape will change according to the quality of grazing and the amount of exercise he is getting.

76   Cubed feeds have added supplements. Giving additional supplements can create an imbalance in the nuitrition and is also a waste of money. When in doubt, check with your veterinarian or feed dealer.

77 If your horse shares a pasture with other horses, arrange with their owners to worm them all at the same time. If you worm yours separately, he will simply ingest eggs and larvae expelled by the other horses.

---

78 It is a false economy to feed cheap, inferior feed. Because the nutritional value is likely to be low, larger quantities must be given, meaning you are not really saving money. If the feed contains dust or fungal spores, it may also be harmful to your horse's health.

---

79 Avoid making saddle soap too wet. If it becomes too lathery, it is less effective at suppling and protecting leather.

---

80   Keep lead ropes neat and safe when they
       are not in use by making a loop just below
       the clip, then winding the rest of the rope
       around the loop. The end can then be
       tucked through the bottom of the loop to
       stop it from coming undone.

81   Shavings can be an expensive form of
       bedding, so keep waste to a minimum by
       placing soiled bedding in a wire basket. The
       clean shavings can be shaken back onto the
       bedding, leaving the manure droppings in
       the basket.

82   Wrap chicken wire around trees in fields to
       stop horses from chewing the bark. Make
       sure the wire is properly fastened and its
       ends bent down to prevent injuries.

83   If hay needs to be fed wet, the best way to
      soak it is to fill a hay net and place it over-
      night in a trough or garbage can full of
      water.

84   An easy way of keeping fetlock hairs
      trimmed and neat is to use a trimming comb
      of the type used for dog grooming that has
      a replaceable razor blade screwed in over
      its teeth.

85   Horses that try to barge out of their stalls
      can be stopped by putting a wooden bar
      across the inside of the door about as high
      as your horse's chest. You will be able to
      duck under to feed and muck out without
      having to open and close the door all the
      time. It will also keep the stall cooler during
      the summer.

86   Hang canvas girths up to dry with the leather parts up so water will not drip on to them.

---

87   A wire-bristled dog grooming comb is very effective for removing dried mud and for getting the loose hairs out of your horse's winter coat. Do not use it on areas where the skin is sensitive.

---

88   Pick out your horse's feet before taking him out of his stall. It saves having to sweep the aisle afterward.

---

89   Put the saddle on from the off (right) side to save having to walk around your horse in order to let the girth down and check that it is not twisted.

90   If your horse returns wet from a ride during the winter, put him in his stall with plenty of dry clean straw beneath his blanket, which should be turned upside down to keep the lining from becoming saturated. Secure everything with a surcingle. The straw lets air circulate and speeds up the drying process, and it will keep him warm so that he does not become chilled.

91   When you are braiding before a show using a needle and threat to secure the braids, save time by threading lots of needles beforehand. Stick them into the front of your sweater or jacket so they're easy to reach.

92   Always keep a list of important numbers next to your telephone, including those of the vet, farrier, and feed dealer. It is quicker in an emergency than going through the telephone directory. Put them into your cell phone directory, too.

93   Bicycle-tire repair kits can be used for repairing rubber riding boots.

94   Wrap some mailing or duct tape, sticky side out, around your hand and use it to remove hairs from your clothing and saddle pads.

95   To prevent a horse from eating his feed too quickly, put a large lump of rock salt in his feed bin. This will also make sure that he receives as much or as little salt in his diet as he wants.

96   After tightening your girth and before mounting, pull each foreleg forward so the skin behind your horse's elbow does not become pinched.

97   Horses with scaly and crusted coats may be treated with an infusion of rosemary. Add approximately half a pint of water to one tablespoon of dried rosemary. Bring it to a boil, cover, and simmer for two minutes. Remove from the heat and, keeping covered, let stand for five to six hours or overnight. Strain off the rosemary and use the liquid as a rinse after shampooing. Check that any skin problem is not due to your not having thoroughly rinsed soap out of your horse's coat after bathing.

98   Use boot polish instead of hoof oil if you are showing your horse in an indoor arena that has shavings in its footing. The shavings will not stick to the hooves.

99 Blankets often have surcingles attached to keep the blanket in place. Prevent the blanket from rubbing by stitching the surcingle to the blanket on either side of the spine, leaving a loop so that pressure is not placed on the horse's backbone.

---

100 Always remove your gloves, however cold the weather, when picking out your horse's feet. It is a good opportunity to detect any signs of heat or swelling in the legs.

---

101 A few stalks of elderberry plant attached to your bridle's browband will help to keep flies away while you are riding. The odor of the crushed stalks repels insects.

102   For a horse who is not very fit and is being brought back into work after a rest, a sheepskin sleeve fitted around the girth will prevent chafing. It can easily be made from a piece of real or synthetic sheepskin. Cut a two- to three-foot piece, stitch it into a tube shape, and slip it over the girth. To reduce the danger of sores or galls, always keep tack well cleaned and supple, saddle pads and girth covers regularly washed, and your horse well groomed.

103   Braid the end of a wispy tail while it is still wet after washing, and wrap the end with an elastic band. When the tail is dry, unbraid it and comb it through with your fingers. This will give the tail a slightly wavy and thicker appearance.

104   To keep a tail out of the way while you are trimming or wrapping hind legs, tie a loose knot in its end.

105   To prevent breaking off hairs, brush out a wispy tail only just after it has been washed. At other times, just work tangles out with your fingers.

106   Wear a stout pair of rubber gloves over woollen ones to keep your hands warm and dry when working around the barn in the winter.

107   If you tend to drop your whip while riding, put an elastic band around its handle and slip your middle finger through it.

108   Feeding garlic can help to control worms, although it should not be used as a replacement for regular worming. Garlic can also help improve skin problems and asthma. Two or three cloves can be crushed and added to your horse's feed.

109   Washing wet, muddy legs with warm water encourages the pores of the skin to open, which allows dirt and bacteria to enter and create infections. If it is necessary to wash legs, use cold water and towel them dry afterward.

110   To keep braids looking neat, use setting lotion instead of water on the mane before making each braid.

111   Adding a double handful of glucose to feed or water will help a horse in shock to recover more quickly. It also helps to reduce the chances of "breaking out" in a sweat again.

112 Snow can pack up into hooves, which may not only make your horse lose his footing but can also strain his tendons. To help repel snow and ice, spray a nontoxic silicon-based grease on to hoof soles. Never smear used engine oil or grease, however, as it could cause damage.

113 Wire and electric fencing can be made more easily visible by tying strips of colored plastic at regular intervals.

114 When putting hay out in the field, place the bales in a sheltered spot so that they are not blown about. Better still, make a hayrack, which will stop the hay from being stepped into the ground and wasted.

115   A little talcum powder sprinkled into close-fitting high leather or rubber boots will make them easier to slip on and off.

116   A horse that tends to eat his bedding will be discouraged from doing so when you thoroughly mix the old bedding with fresh bedding that you have added to it rather than leave it on the top.

117   Always use a quick-release knot when tying up a horse; the free end can be pulled in an emergency and will release instantly.

118   When feeding hay in the field with more than one horse, put one pile of hay more than the number of horses to keep arguments at a minimum.

119 Have two metal discs of the dog tag variety engraved with your name, address, and telephone number, and attach one to your bridle and one to your saddle. Should you have an accident after which your horse runs away, whoever finds him will know whom to contact.

120 Always muck out your trailer after use so it has a chance to air. Soiled bedding can rot the floorboards.

121 Weigh feeds rather than feeding by volume. Some feeds can be deceptive and may vary in weight from one sack to another. Similarly, sections of hay can vary tremendously in weight, and it is easy when feeding by eye either to underfeed or overfeed.

122 Freeze branding has proven to be an effective deterrent against thieves, and it is well worth protecting your horse in this way. Get together with a few friends because there is normally a reduction in price for several horses.

123 Slice carrots lengthways before feeding to reduce the risk of your horse's choking.

124 Build the bedding right up to the stall door to help keep out drafts in winter. If the door does not meet the ground, a thick strip of rubber at its bottom will also help keep drafts to a minimum.

125 When moving straw bedding to your horse's stall, put it into a sack. That will keep you from dropping pieces all over the aisle and ground and having to sweep them up later.

126   Keep a piece of baling twine handy in your pocket when you go trail riding. If your bridle breaks, you now have something with which to make emergency repairs.

127   If you do not have any boot trees, you can help leather boots to retain their shape by stuffing the legs with rolled-up newspaper or magazines.

128   If you are likely to be rushed for time, fill several hay nets beforehand so they are ready for use.

129 When grooming or clipping around the hindquarters of a ticklish horse, hold the tail firmly in your spare hand. If you hold it to one side he will be less inclined to kick out. If he does intend to kick, you will get an early warning by feeling his tail twitching when he becomes cross.

130 Use a summer sheet beneath a stable blanket. Sheets are far easier than blankets to wash and dry when they are dirty.

131 Exercising can be a problem during the winter when there is snow and ice. Construct an arena of soiled hay, straw, or shavings from your horse's stall in a spare corner of the field. Three to four inches deep will provide you with a track on which to walk, jog, trot, or lunge your horse when the weather is really bad.

132   Avoid deep bedding if your horse is prone to respiratory problems, as it can aggrevate them. Also, check with your vet about the advisability of changing the type of bedding.

---

133   When taking photos of your horse, ask someone to squeeze a squeaky toy to attract his attention and encourage him to prick his ears forward.

---

134   Some horses who are hard to clip are upset more by the noise of the machine than its touch. If you think this is the case with your horse, stuff a wad of cotton into his ears.

---

135 If your horse's mane tends to lie on the wrong side, both sides, or, worse still, to stick up, pulling it from the underside will help. Then dampen it with water and braid it loosely, securing the ends of each braid with elastic bands. These stable braids can be left in for a day or so, providing the horse does not rub his mane.

136 Stuff old plastic bags with loose straw and use them as fillers beneath rails when building jumps. They will make the fence more imposing, so you will need fewer poles in order to construct a course. Weight them down with stones to prevent the wind from blowing them away, and staple the ends so that the stuffing does not come out.

137   When turning a horse out into a pasture or corral, leave the gate slightly open so that you can make a quick exit if necessary. Turn his head toward you before letting him go—if he kicks out or bucks on being released, you are less likely to be on the receiving end.

138   If your horse suffers from brittle feet, keep him on bedding made of peat moss.

139   Keep a record of your horse's pulse, temperature, and respiration so that you know what is normal for him. Take note of them twice a year, once during the summer and again during the winter, since they will vary according to the season as well as the horse's age.

140 If your horse has been off work for some time and you are just starting to get him fit again, toughen up the skin in the saddle and girth areas with salt to reduce the chances of sores.

---

141 If you discover that your hay net's drawstring tends to blend in with the net itself, braid up a new one from baling twine of a contrasting color.

---

142 If the keepers on your horse's bridle have stretched and always slide down, hold them in place by putting an elastic band on the cheekpieces just beneath them. When the headpiece straps are placed through the keepers, the elastic bands will hardly be noticeable. and the bridle will look much tidier.

143   Fussy eaters can be tempted by adding molasses to the feed or sprinkling diluted molasses over their hay by using a watering can. Dilute it first in warm water in the proportions of one part molasses to five parts water. Because of its strong aroma and good taste, it can also be used to disguise worming powders or other medicines.

144   Rubber bit guards can be fitted to bits easily by threading two pieces of string through the hole in the middle. Tie each piece with a knot so that two loops are formed; hook one over a tack cleaning hook or door handle, and put your foot on to the other and push downward with it. The rubber will stretch, the round hole becoming an elongated slot through which the bit ring can be passed. The string can then be cut and removed.

145   Rubber riding or Wellington boots that have split around the ankles can be cut down to make useful short waterproof boots for use around the barn.

146   Pull the mane after exercise when your horse is still warm, as the hairs will come out more easily when pores are open.

147   If your horse or pony kicks at his stall door, nail a piece of old carpet or a cloth feed sack stuffed with straw to the inside. He will not injure himself, and the noise will be muffled.

148   When a blanket starts to rub along the shoulders or over the withers, check first that the entire blanket fits as well as possible. Then pad the affected areas with real or synthetic sheepskin, and stitch in a foam rubber pad on either side of the withers. This will raise the blanket a little and keep it from slipping to one side, which can cause rubbing.

149   Rubber overreach boots can be made easier to pull on either by placing them in hot water for a few minutes so that they become more flexible or by smearing a little Vaseline around the tops so that they slide on with less of a struggle.

150   Help prevent thrush by using a lime sock after picking out your horse's feet. A lime sock is made by putting a large handful of garden lime into the toe of an old sock and then tying a knot in the ankle. Hit the sole of the foot with the sock's lime-filled end until the sole is coated with a thin layer of powder.

151   Paint your initials on your grooming kit so that it does not become confused with anyone else's at a multi-owner barn. Use either gloss paint, nail polish, or even the type of enamel used for painting plastic model kits.

152   Clean your felt or velvet-covered hat by brushing it gently with a soft brush to remove dust. Then steam it for a few minutes over the spout of a boiling kettle, and brush gently again to raise the nap and remove any marks.

153   When opening bales of hay or straw, turn the bales so that the knots of the string are on top. Cut at the knots, take hold of them, and pull. The string will slide out easily, leaving you with lengths of string which may come in handy in the future.

154   Metal or plastic garbage cans make useful rodent-proof containers for feed, and will also help protect the contents from dampness. Make certain the covers are a tight fit.

155   A cheap poll guard for traveling can be made by cutting a slit at either end of a rectangular piece of foam rubber, and then slipping the travel halter's headpiece through it.

156　If your horse is clipped at home, install an electrical outlet on a central overhead beam. There will then be far less danger of his standing on the electric clipper cord.

157　If your horse feels the cold during the winter but has to live outdoors, stitch an extra blanket into the lining of his blanket. It can easily be unstictched and removed when the weather becomes warmer.

158　When shipping to a competition, cut up a pair of pantyhose or tights and slip one leg over the tail. Fasten it to your horse's dock to hold it in position. This method will keep the tail clean during the trip.

159   When measuring your horse for a new blanket, take the measurement from the middle of the chest where the blanket would fasten along his side to where it would end at his back. Keep him standing and looking straight ahead, or else the measurement will be incorrect.

───⚜───

160   Have winter blankets repaired in plenty of time before cold and wet weather sets in. If you show up at the tack shop at the last minute, you may find yourself at the end of a long line. Make sure the blankets are clean. If your tack shop does agree to repair dirty blankets, it will probably charge extra for cleaning since mud and grit can damage the sewing machine.

───⚜───

161 A bridle can be kept clean en route to horse shows by being placed inside an old pillowcase. Your own show clothes can be kept inside a dry-cleaning bag until you are ready to change into them.

162 An old table is a handy place to mix feed grains. A metal sweat scraper is equally handy for mixing the grains.

163 If you clip your own horse, use a piece of chalk to mark out the lines of the clip before you start. The chalk guidelines will make for a neater job.

164 Slip feeding instruction in a plastic sleeve and then post on a wall or bulletin board as information for people who will feed your horse when you're away.

165　Keep a bag near your supply of hay or straw and put all the pieces of baling string in it when you remove them from bales. When left lying on the ground, they can easily become mixed up with loose hay or straw and end up in the bedding or in a hay net. If eaten, they can lead to choking. In addition, by placing them safely out of the way, you will always know where to find string when you need it.

166　A good way of stopping a horse from chewing the top of the bottom half of a stall door, as well as to discourage cribbing, is to cut a slit down the length of a piece of tough plastic drainpipe. It should then be slipped the top of the door and nailed at each end. The curved, smooth surface will help prevent the horse's teeth from gripping onto it.

167   If you don't have electricity in your feed room, use a camping lantern. And don't forget to keep a supply of fresh batteries.

168   A horse-proof latch on feed room doors will keep your horse from breaking in and over-eating.

169   Fire extinguishers in tack and feed rooms should be regularly inspected to make sure they're all in working order.

170   Carry a roll of duct tape and a folding knife with which to cut it on trail rides. The tape can be used to wrap a hoof that's lost a shoe and to make emergency tack repairs.

171 Make your own polish to shine brass on harnesses, bridles, and halters with salt or baking soda and vinegar instead of chemical polishes. It's cheaper and better for the environment.

172 Sell unused equipment to raise money for items that you really need. Get together with friends and hold a "paddock sale" just as you would hold a yard sale.

173 Make an effective fly spray by mixing inexpensive antiseptic mouthwash with an equal part water and put in a sprayer. It's safe to use around the horse's muzzle, and horses even seem to like the taste.

174 Fast-food restaurants buy food supplies in five-gallon buckets that they often throw away or will sell for a dollar or two.

175 Vaseline smeared around your horse's eyes will repel flies.

176 To discourage cribbing, hang water buckets and feed tubs low, which will make it much harder for your horse to use them as cribbing edges.

177 Once you've cleaned your barn of cobwebs, wash the walls with a Lysol solution. The mixture does not need to be very strong to discourage spiders and other insects.

178 Finding drowned birds and animals floating in the pasture water trough is not only an unpleasant experience, but they contaminate the water and may deter horses from drinking. Place a small ramp from the water to the lip of the trough to enable the animals to escape.

179   Some thieves have even been known to strip the blankets off horses standing in pastures in broad daylight, although most are more devious. Take preventive measures by writing your name or zip code on blankets with an indelible marker that won't damage the fabric. Mark ID on the roof and side of your trailer too, as this will make it easier to identify and trace if it is stolen.

180   Don't throw away old towels that are no longer fit for use around the house. Instead, save them for jobs around the yard such as drying off a wet horse, tack cleaning, or other uses.

181 If you need to restrict your horse's access to grazing to prevent him from becoming overweight, portable electric fencing can be used to reduce his grazing area. Or you could introduce sheep into your pastures, as they will graze the grass back very short. If neither of these options is feasible, use a bucket muzzle with a mesh bottom. It will limit the amount of grass he can reach to eat, while still allowing him to drink freely.

182 Use a hand-held power-wash at a car wash to help remove ingrained dirt and grime from turn-out blankets—it's quicker, easier and more effective than scrubbing by hand. Transport wet blankets home in a sturdy plastic bag or plastic bin. Make sure the blanket is thoroughly rinsed of any suds.

183   You can easily make a blanket liner for a fraction of the price of buying one. Buy a double- or king-sized duvet at a secondhand sale. They are easy to cut to fit and to sew, adding Velcro for the chest fastenings. Tip: Buy the hollow fiber type of duvet, not the down variety.

---

184   Neck covers are often a better buy than hoods. Horses rarely object to them being put on or taken off, they tear less easily, and they won't interfere with the horse's vision if they slip. You can easily make your own from old blanket materials.

185 If you buy a blanket which has unusual fastenings, buy spares from the manufacturer in case a part breaks, otherwise you may have a long wait if your tack shop has none in stock and needs to order them in specially. An urgent repair job might also lead to a bigger if different fastenings have to be used instead. Tip: If you have blankets with chest fastenings that consist of straps that thread through slots, keep spares of these too, as they often become detached and lost when wet and hung out to dry.

186 A quick, cheap, and easy way of hanging wet turn-out blankets up to dry is to hammer two sturdy nails into your tack room wall; then hang the blanket from them by the metal D's at the back to which the leg straps are clipped. If your blanket doesn't use leg straps, it takes only a few minutes to sew on metal D-rings for this purpose.

187   If you are unsure about your horse's diet, most feed manufacturers now employ nutritionists and have telephone help-lines offering free advice.

~ ♔ ~

188   Garbage cans can make useful feed storage containers, but sometimes larger rodents learn to push off the lids. To prevent this from happening, hook a bungee strap onto one side handle, looping it through the lid handle and then hooking it onto the handle on the other side. If you suspect that someone at your barn is pilfering feed, use a chain with a padlock attached instead.

~ ♔ ~

189   Metal blanket snap fastenings can have an annoying habit of popping undone. Slip a small rubber O-ring or elastic band over the neck of the metal T-bar-shaped fitting before fastening, as this will reduce the amount of play and the likelihood of its accidentally coming undone.

190 Old freezers can be kept or bought cheaply to be used as rodent-proof blanket- or feed-storage chests.

⸺ ♔ ⸻

191 Buy plain jump rails as they are cheaper than painted ones. Paint them yourself by using paint left over from home decorating jobs. The job is made easier if you hammer a six-inch nail into each end of the rail and then hang it between two trestles or jump standards.

⸺ ♔ ⸻

192 Buy a few lengths of ribbon which you can use to braid over the top of your bridle browband for shows. It is cheaper than buying a ready-made one, and you will also be able to get the exact color combinations you want and then change them whenever you wish

⸺ ♔ ⸻

193   Don't throw away damaged old blankets that aren't worth repairing. Any fabric you don't want to keep for repair patches on other blankets can be used to make your own saddle covers, tail guards, and even travel boots. Don't throw away old fleece jackets either, as they can be cut down to make girth covers.

194   Disposable diapers can make useful dressings beneath bandages. They draw discharge away from wounds and keep them dry.

195 Horses are very sensitive to taste, which can lead to them refusing to drink water from a source different to the one they are used to. When traveling to a competition, take your own water supply with you in a large container. If this isn't practical (for example, if you are going to be away from home for several nights), add a little mint flavoring to the water at home to accustom the horse to it—and then add to drinking water as usual when stopping somewhere new, and it will disguise any unfamiliar taste.

196 Many horses traveling long distances will refuse to drink in transit and may become dehydrated. They may be quite happy to nibble at food, however, so offering them a well-soaked hay net will ensure they have some liquid intake.

197   Lengths of gutter cut to size and lined with insulating material make neat coverings for exposed water pipes around the barn. They also ensure that any insulation lagging doesn't get waterlogged or chewed by horses and rodents.

198   A plastic sheet placed over your wheelbarrow when en route to the manure pile will help keep any loose bedding in the manure from blowing away or falling out and making more work for you to do by sweeping up afterwards.

199   Enter horse shows in plenty of time, not only to make sure that the classes you want to enter are not full, but because it's cheaper. "Post" entries made on the day of the show usually cost more than those made in advance.

200   Wear one or even two pairs of tights under your riding pants to help keep warm in cold weather. They won't change the pants' fit too dramatically, and they are very effective against cold weather.

---

201   Wearing knee-highs or cut-down nylon tights makes it easier to get tight-fitting tall riding boots on and off.

---

202   A bag of frozen peas makes a cheap, simple, and reusable emergency ice pack.

---

203   Reduce wasting hay and make it last longer with greedy horses by placing one hay net inside two or three others.

204   Wisping your horse's body is an excellent
      way of improving muscle tone and helping
      to put a bloom on the coat. Make a tradi-
      tional wisp by twisting a rope of hay. They
      are easy to make and cost next to nothing.
      They are also a way of using up instead of
      wasting leftovers from the barn floor, and
      they last a surprisingly long time.

205   Save time cleaning out the back of your car
      or truck if you have to transport hay in it by
      first putting down an old bedsheet, which
      can be lifted and shaken out later.

206   If your horse is upset by the addition of a
      lump of rock salt or a large stone to his feed
      to prevent him from bolting it down, add
      chaff instead, as each mouthful will have to
      be chewed more thoroughly before it can
      be swallowed.

207 Another effective way of preventing a horse from bolting his feed is to sweep clear an area of his stall floor, and then spread the feed across this space to prevent him from taking large mouthfuls.

208 Fill a couple of garbage cans with water during cold spells and leave them close to the barn and pasture troughs. The cans will give you a plentiful supply of water close at hand in the event that pipes freeze.

209 Before making any radical changes to your barn or other buildings, check your local zoning regulations to see whether there are any restrictions or whether you will need to acquire permits from local authorities.

210   Horse blue shampoo that is intended for gray horses will do wonders for getting your dirty saddle pads clean again. Scrub some into the dirty spots, then use it as you would soap liquid in your washing machine.

211   If your horse is hard to catch when you want to bring him in from the pasture, start conditioning him to welcome your approach by feeding him a piece of carrot whenever you're in his stall and whenever you take him out to the pasture. He'll come to associate your presence with treats.

212 Soaking hay can be a problem during freezing weather, so steaming it may be a better alternative. Place either loose hay or a filled hay net inside a sturdy plastic bag and then pour over it one or two pots of water which has just boiled. Tie the neck firmly with a piece of baling string and leave until cool before feeding. Alternatively, put the hay inside a garbage can, add hot water as before, and then place the lid on top. Make sure the hay is shaken out and not left in flakes, or steam from the hot water may not penetrate through.

---

213 Any barn that has boarders should post a list of rules, including safety restrictions, clean-up schedules, and pastures and trails that are off limits to riders and grazers. Keep the list up to date as circumstances warrant.

---

214   Don't rip open shavings bales—open carefully at one end so the bags are left intact. Sturdier than garbage-can bags, they can be used for all sorts of things, such as saving baling twine, storing loose hay sweepings, transporting hay to fields without spilling, steaming hay in, and even for storing blankets.

215   English saddle stirrup leathers are much easier to remove and replace if you first tilt the saddle into a vertical position, with the pommel resting against a firm surface, such as a table. Press down on the cantle and you will find that the stirrup bars will stand slightly away from the tree, making it quick and easy to slide the stirrup leathers off and on.

216   When using brush boots with Velcro fastenings, tape over the tops with duct or insulating tape for extra security.

217 If pulling the tail of a difficult horse, ask someone to hold the horse inside a stall and drape the tail over the top of the lower door while you are pulling so you are not in danger of being kicked. Place a towel over the door first so the sensitive skin under the tail is not damaged.

218 If you have a young horse or an older one who tends to be anxious about certain vehicles on the roads, such as tractors or buses, ask a local riding group whether they would be interested in organizing a traffic training day. You and other interested riders can work on solving these problems in a safe environment with the help of an instructor. By getting a group of people together, the exercise becomes cheaper and more feasible to set up. Horses can also become accustomed during such sessions to other road hazards such as traffic cones, trash bags, and signs.

219 If you tend to get saddle sore, use a seat saver on your saddle; they are also nice and snug to sit on during the cold winter months. You can make one cheaply and easily from an old fleece or foam-filled saddle pad. Wash it thoroughly first, then cut off the flaps and stitch along the raw edges. Attach a piece of elastic that can be slipped beneath the saddle skirts. Also add two long tapes with Velcro at the ends that can be fastened beneath the gullet to help keep everything secure.

220 To discourage your horse from chewing on or leaning against the top of wooden fencing, run a strand of electric fence tape along the top of the length of the pasture's fencing. Since fallen tree limbs and other objects can break the electric connection, check the fencing daily.

221　Urine will soak into stall flooring and create a pungent, unhealthy odor. Hydrologized lime sprinkled over wet spots of dirt floor after the wet bedding has been removed will neutralize the urine's ammonia. Check under rubber stall mats for any soiled bedding that has worked its way there. Scrape the bedding away, and sprinkle with a little hydrologized lime.

222　Use a weigh tape to judge whether your horse is gaining or losing condition. Measure him each week, as your eye is not always the most reliable guide and you tend to notice only dramatic changes rather than more subtle ones. Or you can estimate your horse's weight by the following formula: the horse's heartgirth (measured around the barrel behind the withers and elbow) in inches multiplied by the same number multiplied by the length in inches from center of chest to point of croup divided by 300 will equal the horse's weight in pounds.

223 Save old plastic hypodermic syringes from veterinary visits. Dispose of the used needles safely. Smaller syringes can be useful for cleaning out deep and puncture wounds, and larger ones are handy for administering oral medicines such as cough mixtures.

224 If your horse is reluctant to accept the bit when being bridled, smear the bit with honey, molasses, or even a little mint toothpaste. Also make sure you don't bang his teeth with the bit. This can sometimes happen when unbridling too, particularly with a head-shy horse who may throw up his head; the bit may not only bang against his front teeth, but actually become hooked over the lower ones, panicking him even further. Offer a treat as you remove the bridle—the horse will lower his head and open his mouth for the food, allowing the bit to slide out without difficulty.

225 If bridling up a tall horse who is not very cooperative and puts his head up in the air, to the point where you can't reach it with your hand, use the loop of the bridle head-piece to capture his nose and draw it downward until you can put an arm around it.

226 Make your own horse treats cheaply by drying slices of apple in a low-temperature oven. They will also be free of any additives.

227   Instead of paying for herbal supplements, add herbs to your grazing and let your horse select for himself what he wants. Since herbs can become stifled by grass growth and are also easily destroyed by spraying, clear a path around the edge of the pasture where you can sow them. Herbal seed mixes can be bought from seed dealers and nurseries. Useful herbs to include are ribgrass, chicory, yarrow, dandelion, and sheep's parsley, which are all palatable and rich in essential minerals.

228   Round off square corners of pastures by nailing fencing rails diagonally across them. This will reduce the chances of a horse getting trapped in a corner and being bullied mercilessly by pasture-mates.

229 Moist hay can start to ferment, which not only depletes the hay's nutritional value, but it can lead to spontaneous combustion and barn fires. Check the temperature by putting your hand between flakes; it should feel cool to the touch. Stored hay must be checked frequently. If the hay is warm, check it again with a thermometer. Anything over 150°F is dangerous. In that case, divide the hay into smaller portions, and store in a well-ventilated place.

230 If you are planning to buy a horse, take a camcorder with you when going to see the animal. You can later view the recording at leisure to refresh your memory. You will also have a record of all the seller's replies to your questions so that if a problem later arises, you will have evidence in the event of a legal action.

231　Replacing cheap fittings on blankets with better quality ones may seem like an unnecessary expense, but they will be less likely to bend, break, damage straps, or injure the horse. Any such incident could prove not just inconvenient but very much more costly than replacing the fittings in the first place. Then, save the fittings from old blankets to keep as spares to help reduce repair costs.

232　The quickest and easiest way to clean leather riding gloves is while you are wearing them.

233　Remove leather straps from blankets and sheets before washing. The dye used may bleed and end up discoloring the blanket fabric. If you have to clean the blankets frequently, replace the straps with more washing-friendly nylon ones.

234 Reflective patches onto your horse's turn-out blanket make him easier to spot when you go out to catch him in the field on winter days when it grows dark early. Adhesive dots and strips can be bought separately or you could cut up old reflective vests no longer in good enough condition to wear, and then glue or stitch them on. If several horses are sharing grazing, arrange the patches in different patterns so you can distinguish between them easily and not waste time catching the wrong one.

235 Old broom heads can be used to make a handy mud-remover for your barn and riding boots.

236 Make sure annual "booster" vaccinations are kept up to date, both for the good of your horse's health and because you may be refused entry to a horse show if one has lapsed even if only by as little as a day. Starting the entire course of inoculations over again will also be more expensive than keeping booster shots up to date.

237 New leather boots can sometimes rub and cause blisters. Try using plastic Bubble Wrap packaging in the problem areas, placed inside your socks so it doesn't slip.

238 If you tend to get saddle sore but cannot use a seat saver (in competitions, for example) wear a pair of padded Lycra bicyclist's shorts underneath your riding pants.

239 When trying out a new bridle for size, don't buckle it up—thread all the straps through their keepers instead to avoid damaging the leather; if it doesn't fit it can then be returned without any problem about wear-and-tear. When trying out a saddle, place a piece of thin, clean material such as a dish towel or piece of old bedsheet beneath it. The material will be thin enough to allow you to judge the fit, but will prevent the saddle lining from getting dirty or greasy.

---

240 Hay nets can be awkward to fill if you don't have a helper to hold the top of the net open for you. Make wrestling with uncooperative hay nets a thing of the past by screwing two sturdy hooks into the wall of your hay storage area two feet apart and approximately three feet off the floor. Then simply hang your hay net between the two hooks; use one hand to hold the front edge open, and you'll still have one hand free to fill the net.

---

241 Removing the fillet strings (the straps that go under the tail) from blankets can be a really unpleasant task if your horse tends to soil them, and difficult too if the knots have pulled tight. Sew a pair of metal D-rings to the back of the blanket instead, and then sew a small trigger clip onto each end of the fillet string. These can then be clipped onto the metal D-rings, making the job much easier.

242 Bristles on brooms wear more on the front edge than the back. Rather than throwing them away, extend the broom's life by removing the head and reversing it, so that the back edge becomes the new front edge. Tip: Buying brushes with replaceable heads is also cheaper than buying those with permanently attached handles. When the bristles do finally wear out, you only have to replace the new head, and won't be paying extra for the handle.

243 If the noise made by aerosol or even pump-action type bottles makes your horse anxious when you apply fly repellent, squirt a little onto a body brush or soft cloth instead and wipe it over his coat.

244 Fly repellent may need to be reapplied every few hours for maximum effectiveness, which can be a problem if you are planning a long ride. Make your own fly wipes by spraying repellent onto several squares of cloth, and then placing them in a plastic bag. Tie the neck so that the repellent doesn't all evaporate and the wipes remain damp. The bag can then be slipped into a pocket or saddlebag when you go out for a long ride.

245 Save suitable vegetable and fruit peelings, such as from carrots, parsnips, turnips, cabbage, and apples, when preparing your own meals to add interest to your horse's feed.

246   A single-action apple corer and slicer costs very little to buy but makes slicing apples into small sections ready to add to feed quicker, easier, and safer than using a knife. Knives are also more likely to be "borrowed" for cutting strings on hay and straw bales and for other purposes so they're not around when you need them.

247   Rather than buying expensive stall deodorizer, sprinkle bicarbonate of soda on the floor instead. It kills smells effectively, and is inexpensive and easy to obtain.

248   A wide range of plastic boxes with snap-on lids, which can be bought very cheaply from hardware and drug stores and markets, are ideal for keeping bandages and first-aid kits. They are also good for storing a variety of small objects, such as horseshoe studs.

249 If you use a metal wheelbarrow and find that the tray has rusted away, cut a large plastic oil drum in half lengthwise and bolt it to the chassis to form a new tray.

250 When bringing a horse in from the pasture in the dark, it isn't always practical or safe to lead the horse, open and shut the gate, and hold a flashlight all at the same time. Solve the problem by clipping a front bicycle light onto your belt.

251 Discourage a cribber from chewing the tops of stall doors by securely nailing several stiff-bristled broom heads to them. Cribbing often starts as a result of boredom and/or hunger, so make sure your horse has adequate exercise, turn him out for as long as possible each day, and when he has to be kept in his stall, make sure he has sufficient hay to keep him occupied.

252   While clipping, hairs have a habit of getting everywhere and can be itchy at best and painful if they actually penetrate the skin or get in your eyes. If your shirt or jacket does not have cuffs, slip a rubber band over them at the wrists.

———✦———

253   On very cold nights your horse's water bucket may freeze over. Put the bucket inside a larger one or a cardboard box filled with hay as insulation. Use old sweepings from the hay area that cannot be fed and which would otherwise be thrown away.

———✦———

254   Clothes racks make excellent blanket racks which can be easily moved to one side of the tack room or wheeled outdoors to dry wet blankets. Look for them at secondhand stores or clothing stores that are going out of business.

———✦———

255 Blanket fronts often suffer when horses graze in thorny brush or over fences. Stitch in a leather "apron" over the chest area to prolong the life of the blanket and save on future repairs.

---

256 A handful of salt added to your horse's water bucket after his teeth have been floated will act as an antiseptic mouthwash each time he takes a drink. A saltwater solution is also a cheap and effective antiseptic wash for bathing cuts and injuries.

---

257 If your horse has sensitive skin or has just been clipped, a plastic or Teflon kitchen scourer makes easy work of removing dried mud and sweat from his coat without irritating his skin.

258   Learn reining or dressage tests by drawing out a plan of the arena and then "riding" through it with your fingers at the appropriate places or markers. This is an easy and effective way of learning tests without riding them endlessly on your horse, risking him becoming bored, or anticipating the movements.

259   Keep a supply of homoeopathic remedies for first-aid purposes. If stored correctly they will last almost indefinitely—unlike many "orthodox" drugs which have a limited shelf life—and are therefore more economical.

260   Get together with other owners at the barn to share vets' visits for routine vaccinations and tooth floating—it may cut the cost of the professional's charge for a visit. This procedure often applies to farriers too.

261 Get the maximum value—and benefit—from lessons by asking someone to record you. Later you can replay it and will be better able to appreciate your instructor's corrections. Watching it again before your next lesson will act as a reminder for all the points you need to concentrate on.

---

262 Use a portable knapsack sprayer to spot-treat weeds in a small pasture or paddock. A little goes a long way and saves money on both chemicals and having to hire a professional. Always follow the manufacturer's advice about how long before reintroducing horses after spraying.

263 It's cheaper to buy linseed and other oils for feeding purposes in bulk, but it is awkward lifting and accurately measuring it out of large containers. Using a funnel, pour it into a clean plastic container with a pump dispenser (available from farm stores, or save old shampoo and liquid soap dispensers with this type of top). It will deliver the oil quickly and easily without a mess.

264 Cleaning out barn gutters is time-consuming and may be costly if much debris has been flushed down the drainpipe and clogged up the drainage system. You can buy mesh grids to fit, or better still, you can make your own out of chicken wire. Cut strips that are slightly wider than the gutter diameter, curve them slightly along their length and then place them in the guttering. When you want to clean out the gutters, all you have to do is lift up each length, shake the leaves away, and then replace it.

265 Make a checklist with everything on it that you need for a competition or trip so you don't arrive only to find you have left a vital piece of tack or another item at home. Check everything off as you load it. Tip: Laminate the list (large stationery and office suppliers often offer this service) and use a Magic Marker or felt-tip pen to check off items. After the competition or trip you can then wipe off the check marks with a soft damp cloth and reuse the list.

266 When cleaning your grooming kit, use a horse shampoo to wash brushes rather than household detergent that may irritate your horse's skin.

267 To work shampoo into your horse's coat and thoroughly clean dirt from the roots, work up a lather and then use a rubber curry comb to massage it into the hair with circular movements. If your horse is frightened of hoses, use a watering can instead when giving him a bath.

268 Stop hay from blowing away or being trampled into pasture mud by placing it inside large "muck bucket" plastic containers secured to fence posts (uprights, not horizontal rails) at intervals. Punch holes through the bottom of the containers to prevent them from filling with rain water.

269 Rather than buying several different weights of stall blankets, adding a liner or blanket to a lightweight blanket will make it suitable for really chilly weather, and it is easy to adjust the warmth factor with changes in the weather.

270 Sew extra pockets onto an old kitchen apron: Slip scissors, thread, a comb, and braid bands into the pockets so they are easily to hand when braiding. Push a few pre-threaded needles through the fabric ready for use.

---

271 Make simple saddlebags by sewing pockets on the sides of a saddlecloth to carry sandwiches and other food (and a folding hoof pick) for long trail rides. Use Velcro tape to secure the pocket flaps.

---

272 A chamois leather, lightly dampened, is soft to use on your horse's head when grooming and for removing dust and grease from any area that you cannot groom briskly with a brush. A dampened and well wrung-out chamois leather can also be placed beneath the saddle to reduce the likelihood of the saddle's slipping.

---

273   A tablespoon of cider vinegar added to feed each day will help horses who are growing older and beginning to show signs of stiffness and arthritis.

274   Arthritic horses stiffen up quickly when kept in stalls overnight in cold weather as they can move around less in the confined space. Encourage more mobility by dividing the evening hay into three rations and placing each in different corners of the box, and placing his water in the fourth so he has to move around a little.

275 Lifting a soaked hay net out of water to drain is heavy work. Make it an easier chore by attaching a metal ring to the wall with a sturdy nail below it. When the hay has sufficiently soaked, thread the net drawstring through the ring above and use it as a pulley to lift the net. Once it is out of the water, hook the end of the drawstring over the nail to secure it.

276 Place a folded towel across your horse's forehead when bathing him to prevent water and shampoo getting in his eyes. Tuck each end firmly under the sides of the halter to keep it in place.

277 Keep your hands from slipping on the reins in wet weather by using rubber-covered reins and/or gloves with rubber pimples on the palms.

278　Being stingy with bedding is false economy and you will end up throwing far more away. A deep bed is not only less wasteful, but it offers better protection from scrapes on the stall flooring, and it is also more likely to encourage your horse to lie down when resting.

279　If your horse is frightened by clippers, even if you don't have your own set you can still spend some time getting him used to the idea. Start by running a hand-held car vacuum-cleaner near his stall, then run it inside the stall once he has grown accustomed to the sound, and gradually move closer it until you can run it all over his body.

280   If your horse has a back problem, check his blankets as well as the fit of his saddle. Blankets are often overlooked but can be a significant source of such problems, and if they are not a good fit, they will certainly contribute to any existing discomfort.

---

281   When finishing up a hand-pulled mane, use rubber thimbles and/or washing-up or rubber surgical gloves to give your fingers a better grip on the hair and prevent blisters.

---

282   When handling a nervous horse, scratch his neck and along the crest with your fingertips rather than giving hearty pats. The horse will find the action far more soothing and less aggressive.

---

283   Top off water buckets with a kettleful of hot water in the winter. If you don't have a kettle, use a Thermos bottle of hot water instead. This will not only delay the bucket freezing over, but will encourage your horse to drink—many horses will reduce their intake if the water is too cold and may suffer dehydration as a result.

284   Stall bandages can provide extra warmth in cold weather, the equivalent of adding an extra blanket. They are useful if a horse is old or ill and weak when you may not want to put the extra weight of blankets on his back.

285 You don't need a lot of jumps in order to be able to practice riding courses. Build a Y-shaped grid of jumps using three sets of fences. They can be continuously jumped in either direction—you can make turns wide and easy, or tighter to practice jump-off tactics.

286 Animal hair that becomes stuck to your clothing is easy to remove with a rubber dish-washing glove. Put it on, dampen it slightly, and "brush" the fabric briskly with your hand. The hair will stick to the glove and can be rinsed away in a bowl of warm water.

287 Before turning a new horse out in the field with others, first take it for a ride with the most dominant horses to give them all a chance to get safely acquainted, which will reduce the likelihood of the newcomer being bullied.

288   A quick and easy way to clean all the green algae from the sides of a pasture water trough is with a piece of nylon garden netting. Scrunch it into a large ball and use it as a giant scouring pad.

---

289   Dangerously sharp edges may be exposed on metal salt and mineral block holders as the block wears down, especially when some horses crunch their way through these licks at a rapid rate. Instead, use cylindrical rather than brick-shaped blocks. They have a hole through the middle instead: thread a piece of stout rope or braided baling string through the hole and hang so that it swings freely. That will not only be safer but it will prevent waste and provide entertainment as a toy.

290 Rubber car floor mats will cut stall draft: Cut in half and nail to the bottom edge of stall doors, then screw (not nail) a thin lath of wood over the top to secure. Old mats can be bought at auto junkyards, or you may be replacing your own.

---

291 Instead of buying an expensive preprinted logbook or equine Filofax in which to record your horse's health record, make your own. Ring binders have sturdy covers. It is easy to add additional information and details, and there are no problems of running out of space. The binder can be given to a new owner if you sell the horse. Keep conformation photographs of your horse in your folder, taken from both sides plus front and rear views. In the event of his being stolen these can help to make identification and recovery easier. Make sure your photographs are kept up to date.

292   Mucking-out equipment is expensive to replace, so store it properly. Keep brooms and pitchforks under cover where the handles will not become rotted by rain. Avoid leaning on broom handles as it will bend and damage the bristles. Prolong the working life of wheelbarrows by standing them on end when not in use, otherwise rainwater will collect in the pan and rust it.

293   Clipper oil can cause irritation and blistering on sensitive skin, so keep a cloth handy (an old dish towel is ideal) for wiping off excess oil each time you lubricate the blades and before resuming your clipping. Brush off loose hair after clipping so the hair does not stick to blanket lining and cause irritation, then wipe over clipped areas with a damp sponge to remove any last small traces of clipper oil from the coat.

294 Keep hairy legs, fetlocks, and heels trimmed in winter as trimming will make it quicker and easier to dry them. In addition, in very severe freezing conditions wet hair will not form uncomfortable little icicles around trimmed fetlocks. Dense hair, which tends to hold in moisture, creates warm damp conditions ideal for bacteria to thrive in, so it may be more likely to lead to problems such as cracked heels and mud fever. If hair is kept trimmed, these problems are less likely to occur, but if they do, you will be better able to spot the problem early. Tip: When trimming, leave just a small tuft of hair at the ergot to help channel water away from the heels.

295   A horse toy is easily made from a large plastic milk jug. Remove and dispose of the cap, and then half fill with water, adding a few drops of peppermint essence to add an interesting smell. Loop a length of braided baling string through the handle and hang up in your horse's stall so that it can swing freely. Out in the pasture, horses will enjoy a soccer or plastic traffic cone to play with. Such toys may distract them from damaging other more valuable items such as fencing or trees.

296   A little bit of baby oil brushed through your horse's tail after washing will help mud slide out of it during winter, making it easier to care for the tail without breaking or damaging the hairs.

297 After washing a tail, grasp the hair just below the end of the tail bone and twirl them briskly around in a circle. This quickly gets rid of excess water, although you may soak someone standing nearby!

298 Smear vegetable cooking oil onto your hands and then rub them over your horse's legs, belly, and inside his hind legs to help prevent mud from sticking during the winter. The mud will come off easily when dry. Apply the oil when your horse is clean and dry; do not put it on top of mud or apply when your horse is wet, or else it will trap rather than repel moisture. Vaseline or baby oil can be used if preferred.

299   You will probably spend less time riding in winter than in summer. Especially if you have a particularly severe spell of weather that puts a stop to your riding, take advantage of the opportunity to do such chores as having your saddle re-padded and giving your horse vaccinations, which might normally interfere with your riding activities.

300   To help lift grease from the coats of clipped horses and reduce the chance of infection, pour hot water into a bucket (make sure the water is not scalding—it should be no hotter than you can tolerate on your own skin) and add a few drops of lavender or tea tree essential oil. Soak a clean towel into the water, and then wring it out so it is damp. Rub firmly over the coat in a circular motion, rinsing and squeezing out after every few circles.

301 Hay nets often swing around as horses eat and end up with a tightly twisted drawstring that's hard to remove quickly and easily. Fit a sturdy hook with a narrow gap (the type with a blunt hook end) from which you can hang your net. When you want to remove it, simply slip the drawstring over the end of the hook.

302 Use an old colander to clear debris from pasture water troughs. Colanders are also good during winter to remove chunks of ice from troughs after you have broken them up.

303 A colander or mesh sieve can be used to scoop out soaked sugar beets and add to concentrate feeds. Any remaining liquid can then be sprinkled over hay to entice fussy eaters or given simply as a treat. Tip: Coarse mixes are also good for encouraging fussy feeders to eat as the mixes contain molasses, which makes them more tempting.

304 Hedgerows and pasture edges should be checked regularly for poisonous plants that often thrive in such habitats. Unless you are an expert botanist, identifying such plants isn't easy, so take a pocket field guide that shows the plants in their various stages of growth.

305 Plastic oil drums cut in half lengthways can form fillers for show jumps or cross-country fences. They are light and easy to move around, they won't rot or rust, and they will not roll if they are placed with their cut edges on the ground.

---

306 A large plastic oil drum cut in half lengthways makes a pasture water trough or hayrack. It is also a suitable container in which to soak several hay nets at the same time. Place the drum on heavy scrap lumber to prevent it from rolling over.

---

307 The plastic sterile covers in which large syringes are packed make a useful receptacle for your hoof-dressing brush. Nothing else in your grooming kit will become oily.

308   Ease the discomfort caused by a young horse's teething by rubbing a little preparation intended for children teething into his gums.

309   Make a fly net if your horse is prone to eye infections from summer insects and a fly fringe doesn't provide sufficient protection. Use netting from vegetable or fruit bags or a piece of window curtain netting. Sew Velcro tape along the edges so that it can be wrapped around the halter cheekpieces (and be easily removed when not needed) and then add two lengths of plain tape or ribbon to the top corners. Punch two holes in the halter headpiece, one on either side, and slightly above the height of the eyes. (To gauge where the holes should go, mark their positions with a pen while the halter is on your horse.) The tapes are then threaded through these holes so the net doesn't slip down.

310 When trotting a horse to determine lameness, don't hold the lead rope so tight that you restrict his head carriage. The movement may be an indicator of which leg the horse is lame on. Remember also to turn the horse away from you rather than toward you, so don't block the view of the observer. It's safer, too, as your toes won't be stepped on.

---

311 If your horse finds mane-pulling uncomfortable, first rub a little oil of cloves into his neck at the base of the mane; the oil will make the skin less sensitive. Wear rubber gloves so your own fingers don't go numb.

312   Nose nets can help in some cases of head-shaking brought on by pollen allergies by acting like a filter. They are simple to make using the toe end from one leg of a pair of stocking or pantyhose. Trim it to the right length and slide it over the muzzle. The remaining top end of the leg can be used to make soft ties with which to attach the net to the bridle's noseband to keep it in place.

313   Full-length waxed slickers or coats are perfect for riding in wet weather, but their inside leg straps that hold the coat close to your legs can sometimes cause problems when dismounting—the one on your right leg can occasionally get caught on the saddle's cantle. Replace the buckle with a Velcro fastening that will come undone if this happens.

314   If you have to put hay out in a hay net in the pasture in winter and there is nowhere more suitable to hang it than on the pasture's fence, make sure that when it is empty the net will not dangle dangerously low where your horse's feet may become tangled in it. Tie the drawstring to the fence as usual, then tie a second string to the net's bottom and thread this length through net holes and around the horizontal rail so that the net lies lengthwise rather than hanging vertically.

---

315   Should your horse be difficult about having his head clipped, make a bridle path instead. Slip on the bridle to act as a guideline, and clip the lower half of the head up as far as the cheekpieces on each side; most horses will accept this more readily and it looks better than leaving the whole head unclipped.

316   The keepers of full-cheek snaffle bits often have a habit of getting lost. If you lose one and don't have a spare, temporarily make do with a rubber band or an elastic hair band. Slip it over the bridle cheekpiece billet, then twist tightly until just enough slack is left to slip over the end of the bit cheekpiece to hold it in place.

317   Use battery-operated dog trimming clippers for clipping your horse's head. Facial hair is finer than body hair so it doesn't matter if the motor is less powerful, and it is a comparatively small area anyway. These clippers are usually much quieter and vibrate less so the horse is less likely to object, and as the blades are narrower it is easier to work around all the little awkward areas.

318 The easiest and quickest way to roll a bandage is to lay the Velcro tape end against your thigh and then roll downward, using your thigh as a support. This technique makes sure you have a firm rather than loose and a fairly consistent pressure as you roll, which will make it easier to put on correctly tensioned bandages later. Make sure you lay tapes to the inside of the bandage as you roll, so that the Velcro will be on the outside when you bandage your horse.

319 Keep old English stirrup leathers because they make good neck straps.

320 It is not ideal to leave a halter on your horse while he is out in the pasture because there is a danger that he could get caught up on fencing. However, sometimes it is necessary for horses that are difficult to catch or if you need to use a fly scrim or nose guard. In this case, minimize the risk by using a lightweight leather halter, which—unlike nylon—will snap if the horse does accidentally get caught.

321 Putting on a tail bandage is easier if you stand close and to one side of your horse's hindquarters and rest the tail bone over the top of your shoulder. Your horse cannot then clamp his tail down, and you have both hands free to bandage with.

322 Rodent control can be a problem around barns; traps aren't always very effective, and poison can be a danger to other animals and young children. Try a natural deterrent such as one or two barn cats, which will also provide company for your horse when he's in his stall.

323 Horses with white or pink muzzles often suffer from sunburn during the summer. Nonallergenic total sunblocks are effective but they need to be reapplied several times during the day for maximum effectiveness. This can be expensive and time-consuming if you own more than one horse. An alternative is to make a nose guard to protect against the sun: Simply make a rectangular flap of heavy fabric and attach it to the halter noseband with Velcro tapes.

324   Replace tie tapes on leg wraps and bandages with Velcro for quicker and easier bandaging. They are also safer as it won't be possible to over-tighten them and cause damage to tendons and ligaments. Bandages should always be additionally secured for safety. Since stitching is time-consuming and awkward, especially if the horse is fidgety, use duct tape.

325   Don't have rubber reins recovered more than twice. The repair person can't use the same stitch holes each time and, as a result, the leather will become weakened.

326   Lunge reins always seem to acquire knots that pull tight and are almost impossible to undo again. The easiest way to unravel one is to use a hoof pick to push into the knot and then loosen it to the point where your fingers can tease it out. The blunt hoof pick point will not cut into and thus damage the rein.

327   If you have trouble keeping both reins the same length when riding, slip a brightly colored rubber band over each rein at the same distance from the bit so you can judge both accurately and instantly.

328 Stand on a heavy box when braiding so that mane hairs are drawn upward into the braid rather than out sideways. This will enable you to make sure that any shorter hairs are incorporated into the braid for a tighter and neater braid, avoiding a saggy, untidy, and amateurish appearance. Don't wash the mane or tail just before you want to braid or pull it as the hairs will be slippery and hard to hold.

329 Convert a plain cavesson noseband into a dropped/flash noseband by securely stitching a loop of nylon web around the noseband front; then slip a leather strap through the loop. It may not be fancy enough for competition wear, but is quite adequate for schooling and other general riding purposes, and it is easy to remove. Suitable leather flash straps can be picked up secondhand or from tack shops at less than the cost of a new noseband, and if you later decide you want to keep it like this, you can ask a tack repairer to stitch in a nicer-looking leather loop to hold the strap.

330 When washing towels used for drying horses, don't add fabric conditioner. While it may make the towels softer and fluffier, they will also be less absorbent.

331   Safety-pin or tape a piece of fabric or tissue soaked with fly repellent to the peak of your hat while riding so that you as well as your horse can enjoy fly-free rides during the summer.

---

332   If you do not wish to remove the reins from your horse's bridle while lungeing, make sure they are out of way so they cannot slip over his head or dangle down dangerously near his front legs. Do so by twisting them around each other under his neck and then putting them up through the throatlatch of either his bridle or lungeing cavesson.

---

333   After cleaning water troughs, add a dash of mint mouthwash to freshen them up and camouflage the lingering odor or taste of any disinfectants that have been used.

---

334 If your horse dislikes having his mane pulled, try pulling the hairs out in an upward, rather than sideways, direction. This technique is less painful.

---

335 To prevent neatly rolled bandages from unraveling and getting in a tangle, slip a rubber elastic band over the roll.

---

336 Stop bristles on the sides of dandy brushes from becoming squashed and broken by nailing a piece of leather to the sides where your fingers normally hold the brush.

---

337   If you try to add extra holes to a nylon web halter by using an ordinary hole punch, you'll find it difficult to do and the holes will tend to fray. Save yourself the expense of buying a hole-riveting kit (which you probably won't need to use very often anyway) by first finding a nail of the same diameter as the hole you wish to make. Holding it securely in a pair of pliers, heat the nail until very hot and then poke a hole through the nylon strap with the hot point. The nail will go through easily, and the heat will seal the edges of the hole to prevent fraying.

338   When first introducing a young horse to the bit, use either a rubber or rubber-covered bit initially so that it is less frightening for him if, despite your taking care, the bit's mouthpiece bangs his teeth. Alternatively, if you prefer to use a metal bit, wrapping some Vetrap around the mouthpiece will cushion the teeth and also make the bit feel less cold in his mouth.

339   Keep stored blankets and tack free from dampness by placing them inside cotton pillowcases (which will "breathe") and then storing them inside containers in which you've placed packets of silica gel.

340   Small gaps in stalls that let in drafts can be effectively and cheaply blocked with tightly rolled sheets of newspaper.

341   Horses who have learned to remove their halters by rubbing them off over one ear can be foiled by your making two cotton or nylon web loops, and slipping one over the headpiece and one over the throatlatch. Cut down an old stirrup leather and buckle it snugly around the horse's neck just behind his ears so that it forms a second throatlatch, threading it first through the loops attached to the halter.

342   Store bales of hay off the ground to prevent them from becoming damp. Instead of paying for wooden pallets, old car tires will do the job just as well. They can be obtained either free or for next to nothing from garages and auto junkyards.

343   Braid three strips of nylon tights, stitch one end firmly to your horse's blanket, and sew a clip on to the other end to make tough but non-chafing leg straps.

344   When clipping, use a length of baling string twine to check that the clip's height is the same on each side.

345 Old vegetable racks can make excellent shelving containers for such tack room items such as tack-cleaning products, grooming items, and for odds and ends. To keep them out of reach of small children or other animals in the barn, you can easily hang them high up on a wall.

---

346 If your horse tends to puff out his belly while you are tightening the girth, feed him a handful of hay and then try again while he is still munching.

---

347 Place unrolled bandages inside an old pillow-case before putting in the washing machine to help prevent them knotting themselves around other items.

348   A nicely effective way to display your horse show ribbons is to take a length or two of wide ribbons, perhaps in the barn's colors, and stitch a curtain ring to one end. The prizes can then be tied or pinned to the ribbon, with the curtain ring used to hang them up from a nail or hook screwed into the wall.

349   When cleaning machine-washable girths, buckle the tongues in place and keep them from becoming wedged in the washing-machine drum holes by wrapping pieces of wire around them to keep them from becoming unbuckled.

350   Put metal bits and stirrup irons in the dish-washer—they'll come out looking brand new.

351   Dividing your horse's mane into wide bunches and securing them firmly with rubber bands close to the crest so that the mane stands upright makes it faster and easier to see what you are doing when clipping your horse's neck, as well as to clip close to the root line.

352   Old toothbrushes make ideal small brushes for getting into tight areas when cleaning out hairs that clog up clippers and clipper blades.

353   Use the rough side of an old dishpan scourer to quickly and easily remove dried saliva from bits and to restore a bright finish.

354   Keep a small nail, a box of toothpicks, or a box of wooden safety matches handy in the tack room to remove soap and dirt from clogged-up holes in stirrup leathers, bridles, and halters.

355   For a quick, clean, and easy way to apply hoof oil just before a horse show class, take an empty shoe-shine bottle with a foam applicator pad, wash it out thoroughly, and when dry fill it with hoof oil. Press the foam pad onto a piece of paper a few times until the oil flows, and it's ready for use. Screw the top on firmly to make sure the pad stays moist.

356 If your horse learns how to untie himself by pulling at the knot of his lead rope, attach a longer rope than usual to his halter, thread it through the normal tie ring, and then on to a second ring set to the side where he can't reach it. Tie it, as usual, to a piece of breakable string.

357 A small lock de-icer is inexpensive, lasts a long time, and is small enough to fit easily into a pocket. It is invaluable for de-icing frozen pasture and barn padlocks in winter.

358 Use combination padlocks on field gates and buildings if there are many people at the barn. The cost is less than that of having lots of keys cut, and there are no worries about losing keys.

359   Don't throw away old nail brushes. Use them for jobs such as scrubbing grease off synthetic girths when hand-washing them and for removing dirt from the soles and welts of riding boots.

360   After your farrier leaves, use a magnet attached to a stick to "sweep" the area around where he or she had been working. You're likely to find discarded or leftover nails that way.

361   Keep ten-foot lengths of strong rope in the tack room in case you and/or helpers must get a horse that is cast in his stall up on his feet.

362　The rope by which you tie your horse should be no lower than the height of his withers, and the rope should not be long enough to let his head reach the floor or ground. Otherwise, he may step on or over the rope.

363　Picking out your horse's feet every day, or even more frequently, will alert you to any loose shoes, a stone caught in the foot, or the beginning of thrush.

364　To reduce the chance of fire and to eliminate breeding grounds for insects and rodents, keep at least a thirty-foot perimeter regularly mowed around your barn and any other buildings and structures near it or in your pasture.